Mama pulled ONE fat tomato from the garden today.

one
1!

1

Tony tugged TWO golden carrots from the garden today.

two
2 ..

2

Sarah scooped up THREE red cabbages from the garden today.

three
3
....

3

Harry hauled FOUR heads of lettuce from the garden today.

Dad grabbed FIVE bunches of broccoli from the garden today.

7

Piper plucked SIX juicy strawberries from the garden today.

9

Grandpa picked SEVEN outstanding onions from the garden today.

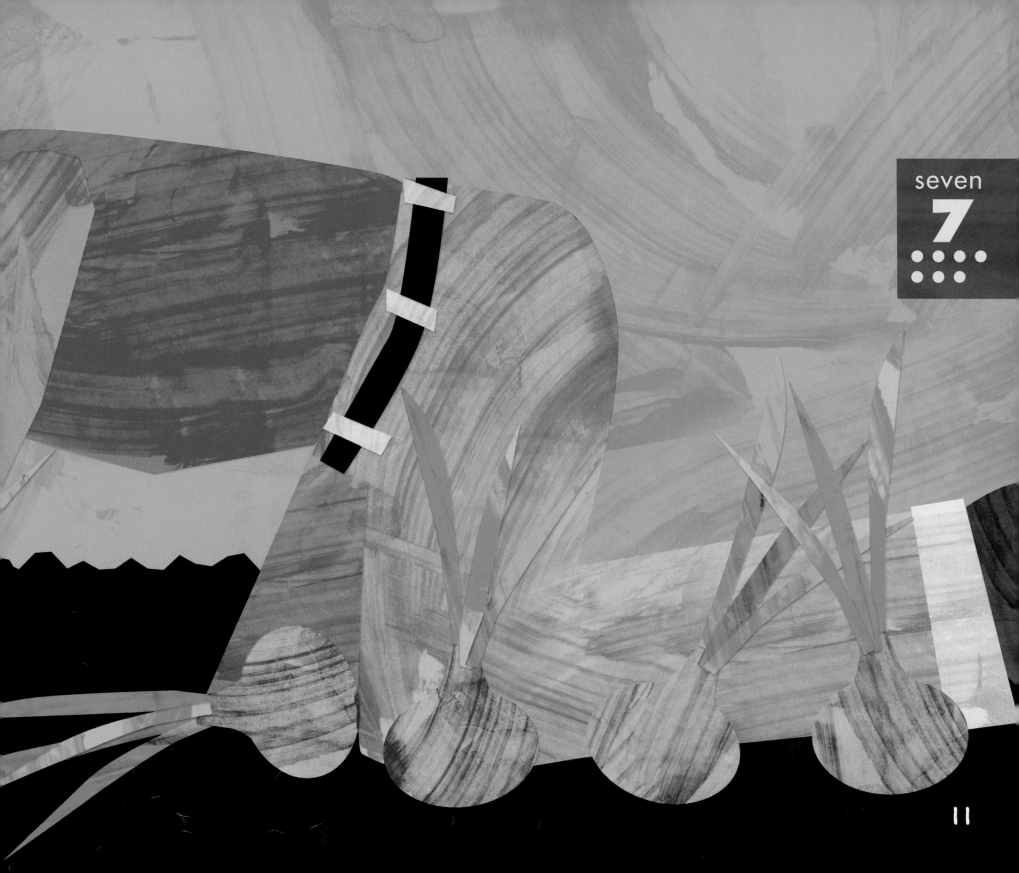

12

Grandma gathered EIGHT pods of peas from the garden today.

eight
8

Carl collected NINE cool cucumbers from the garden today.

nine
9
••••
•••
••

15

The twins rooted up TEN ripe radishes from the garden today.

Radish

10

ten
**10**

18

I carried ELEVEN perfect peppers from the garden today.

eleven
11

Now the family has TWELVE plates
of spectacular salad

from the garden today.

twelve
**12**

# Fun Facts

 There are more than 4,000 different kinds of tomatoes!

 The orange part of the carrot is the plant's root.

 Red cabbage has leaves that are reddish-purple. The most popular cabbage is white cabbage, which has light green leaves.

 People have been growing lettuce for thousands of years. People in Persia may have been the first to have lettuce farms, in 550 B.C.

 Broccoli only takes about 110 days to grow from a seed into the broccoli you can eat.

 Strawberries belong to the same plant family as roses do.

 When cut, a raw onion can give off a vapor that makes people's eyes water.

 The peas inside a pea pod are seeds.

 Cucumbers grow on a hairy vine. The vine's leaves are shaped like triangles.

 Some radishes are round and red. Others are white and look like icicles. They also can be yellow, pink, purple, and black.

 Many people eat green bell peppers. But if the green bell peppers are left on the plant longer, they turn other colors, such as red, yellow, or purple.

 Salads can be made of many things—vegetables, fruit, and even pasta!

# Find the Numbers

Now you have finished reading the story, but a surprise still awaits you.

Hidden in each picture is one of the numbers from 1 to 12. Can you find them all?

Key

**1** –stem of tomato

**2** –in Tony's right ear

**3** –holding girl's ponytail

**4** –on the wagon's handle

**5** –on the broccoli that is highest on the page

**6** –on the basket's handle

**7** –on shirt collar

**8** –earring

**9** –back of cap

**10** –on radish row marker

**11** –on farthest right yellow pepper

**12** –in top left salad on page 21

# Go on an Observation Walk

Counting is fun! Step outside your door, and practice counting by going on an observation walk in your neighborhood—or even in your own yard. Ask an adult to go with you. On an observation walk, you notice the things all around you. Count the number of trees in your yard or on your block. Count the number of dogs you see. Count the number of windows on one side of your home. You can count everything!

# Glossary

**cucumber**–a long, green vegetable that grows on a vine and is filled with seeds

**pod**–a long case that holds the seeds of some plants

**radish**–a small red and white vegetable that grows in the ground

**root**–the part of a plant that grows under the ground

**vapor**–a gas

# Index

# On the Web

## Fact Hound

Fact Hound offers a safe, fun way to find Web sites related to this book. All of the sites on Fact Hound have been researched by our staff.
*http://www.facthound.com*

1. Visit the Fact Hound home page.

2. Enter a search word related to this book, or type in this special code: 1404805788.

3. Click on the FETCH IT button.

Your trusty Fact Hound will fetch the best sites for you!

## Acknowledgments

Thanks to our advisers for their expertise, research, and advice:

Stuart Farm, M.A.
Mathematics Lecturer,
University of North Dakota
Grand Forks, North Dakota

Susan Kesselring, M.A.
Literacy Educator
Rosemount-Apple Valley-Eagan
(Minnesota) School District

The editor would like to thank Barbara Stendahl, Master Gardener coordinator for the University of Minnesota Extension Service–Dakota County, for her expert advice in preparing this book.

Managing Editor: Bob Temple
Creative Director: Terri Foley
Editor: Brenda Haugen
Editorial Adviser: Andrea Cascardi
Copy Editor: Sue Gregson
Designer: Nathan Gassman

Page production: Picture Window Books
The illustrations in this book were rendered digitally.

Picture Window Books
5115 Excelsior Boulevard
Suite 232
Minneapolis, MN  55416
1-877-845-8392
www.picturewindowbooks.com

Printed in the United States of America.

**Library of Congress Cataloging-in-Publication Data**
Dahl, Michael.
From the garden : a counting book about growing food / written by Michael Dahl ; illustrated by Todd Ouren.
p. cm. — (Know your numbers)
Summary: Introduces the numbers from one to twelve as family members pick a variety of vegetables from the garden. Readers are invited to find hidden numbers on an illustrated activity page.  Includes bibliographical references and index.
ISBN 1-4048-0578-8 (reinforced lib. bdg.)
1.  Counting—Juvenile literature. 2.  Vegetables—Juvenile literature.
[1. Counting. 2. Vegetables. 3. Picture puzzles.] I. Ouren, Todd, ill. II. Title.
III. Series: Dahl, Michael. Know your numbers.
QA113.D33 2004
513.2'11—dc22
2003020940